HANDBOOK ON

PSYCHIATRIC CASUALTIES IN BATTLE

FOR MEDICAL OFFICERS

1951

The Naval & Military Press Ltd

Published by

The Naval & Military Press Ltd

Unit 5 Riverside, Brambleside
Bellbrook Industrial Estate
Uckfield, East Sussex
TN22 1QQ England

Tel: +44 (0)1825 749494

www.naval-military-press.com
www.nmarchive.com

CONTENTS

PSYCHIATRIC CASUALTIES IN BATTLE

CHAPTER 1

HISTORICAL

The psychiatric casualty in battle is the soldier who becomes ineffective as a direct result of his personality being unable to stand up to the stresses of combat. Psychiatric disabilities led to large losses in effective manpower in World Wars I and II. In World War I, the problem became acute in 1916 when, during the first battle of the Somme, several thousand soldiers were evacuated from the front within a few weeks owing to " shell-shock ". There was no specific medical organization to deal with the problem, and it was considered impossible to distinguish between cases of psychoneurosis and those of malingering. It was thought that the setting up of special treatment centres for these cases would result in the development of a " backward-looking " attitude among forward troops with resulting uncontrollable wastage of manpower.

The problem, however, persisted, and towards the end of 1916, a number of neuro-psychiatrists were commissioned and a number of treatment centres were established in base areas in France. Experience in the handling of cases in these centres showed that a large number of cases might have been returned to duty earlier had it been possible to have treated them for a few days during an earlier stage of the illness at a more forward centre. In 1917, special treatment centres for these cases with a specialist officer at each centre were established in the army areas in France. Results of treatment which were very disappointing after evacuation to England were surprisingly good in these more forward centres, and in some over 60 per cent. were reported to have been returned to duty, mainly to fighting units. The unfortunate term " shell shock" was in universal use and applied alike whether the breakdown occurred in the combat zone or in rear areas, and whether the true disability was psychosis, psychoneurosis or mental deficiency. The term implied that the condition was attributable to an organic injury sustained as a result of blast, etc., and was therefore morally justified. Over 100,000 pensions were granted for psychiatric disabilities incurred in World War I. In 1920, the Southborough Committee surveyed the psychiatric problems of World War I with a view to recording for future use the expert knowledge gained of these disabilities during the war. The Committee, after sifting the evidence of combatant and medical officers, produced a series of recommendations, the majority of which still have the full approval of informed psychiatric opinion. The report stressed the importance of careful selection and the promotion of good morale through adequate training and skilled leadership in the prevention of these casualties. During World War II, the proportion of psychiatric casualties in battle to total battle casualties varied between 5 and 30 per cent. In the North West European Campaign a total of 13,255 psychiatric casualties occurred. These casualties, therefore, continued to present a considerable problem, much of which was avoidable.

CHAPTER 2

AETIOLOGY

This may be considered from three different aspects. Listed in the order of their relative importance these are :—

(a) The individual.

(b) The group.

(c) The environment.

The Individual

A faulty previous psychiatric history was found to be the most important single predisposing factor in those who broke down in World War II. An important factor resulting in psychiatric casualties in a unit is the presence in the unit of unstable men who are not suited for combatant duties. There are some men who will not become good combatant soldiers no matter how thorough their training and how good their leadership. Many soldiers, however, have a predisposition to breakdown, but do not do so. They are effective in combat and remain so over long periods. The individual success or failure depends largely upon the unit of which the soldier becomes a member, and upon his leader. A good leader enables him to utilize what assets he has. It is impossible, therefore, to predict with any degree of success all soldiers who are likely to breakdown in battle, no matter how good their selection. A battalion which contains good officers and N.C.Os., and in which morale and pride of regiment are high, can successfully carry a proportion of men of moderate or indifferent quality. On the other hand, psychiatric breakdown in battle also occurs in reasonably sound personalities with stable past histories. Men of low intellectual endowment seldom make good soldiers in modern warfare. The emotional strains to which the soldier is subjected in modern warfare and the tasks he has to perform are very different from those in earlier wars. Fear has now become more prolonged, and, in addition, there is often worry over the safety of the family at home in air raids. The mental defective no doubt acquitted himself well in the wars of the 18th and 19th centuries but finds it very difficult to withstand the many stresses which are an essential part of modern warfare.

Few soldiers think of war aims on national terms. Many have only accepted the necessity of leaving home in order that the home may be preserved for their return. While overseas, mail from home is the soldier's one emotional link with that home and he expects to keep in touch with it. If he has domestic worries, and many soldiers overseas have such worries, they are not always founded on fact or on reason, but have often been influenced by long delays in the mail service. Regular arrival of mail is a most effective bulwark against insidious infiltration of deep seated anxiety about home. Its importance cannot be over estimated, and it is almost as important to the soldier's mental health as is food to his physical health. During 1940 and 1941, there was a great deal of anxiety among members of the Middle East Force concerning the bombing at home, and, unfortunately at this time when news from home was desperately important to the soldier, his mail was often scarce and irregular. If, however, a soldier's worries about home are founded on fact and he learns of his wife's infidelity, then he feels that he has been misled. What he is fighting for may then have crumbled before the fight is over.

The Group

The relationship between an officer and his men is the key to conduct in battle, and the most important factor in reducing the number of psychiatric casualties is good individual unit leadership. Other things being equal, the psychiatric breakdown rate in battle provides an index of the quality of a unit's leadership. When the latter is faulty, the soldier at once feels insecure, and bad leadership is to be suspected whenever a large number of psychiatric casualties arrive simultaneously at a medical centre from one unit without well confirmed evidence of exceptional stress. If the officer breaks, his men will break. The same feeling of insecurity is stimulated by inadequate training. The hastily trained soldier who finds himself in action after an insufficient grounding in his craft and without confidence in his ability to use his weapons under battle conditions is prone to breakdown. It is confidence in ability to use a weapon under battle conditions which is generally lacking. Technical mastery of a weapon alone is not enough.

The broader issues of war are meaningless to many soldiers. Generally, the strongest forces which keep men going in battle are regard for their comrades, respect for their leader and the reputation of their unit, and their own self respect. To a large extent these depend on the bonds existing between themselves and their fellow soldiers. They fight for something rather than against something. Many psychiatric casualties in battle occur a few days after joining a new unit, and many give a history of a recent change of unit either as a result of having been sick or wounded or of having arrived recently in a draft from home. They break down before they have had time really to know their officers and N.C.Os. It takes time for most men to become integral parts of new units, to develop loyalties and to identify themselves with their new unit as members and not as outsiders. Until this happens, the individual soldier is always vulnerable when exposed to stress and those with an inherent predisposition to breakdown are exceptionally so. A unit that has suffered a very large number of wound casualties consists to a large extent of reinforcements. A high psychiatric casualty rate may be expected since the emotional ties among the men and between the men and their officers which is the most important single factor in preventing breakdown are as yet insecure. Some reinforcement establishments and transit camps played a part in the causation of psychiatric breakdown in World War II. The sense of frustration which affected most men who had to remain in them for any length of time, often in idleness and uncertainty, made them only too often become centres of low morale. In the North West European campaign during the first quarter of 1945, a large proportion of psychiatric casualties breaking down on the battlefield were reinforcements. **Assimilation of reinforcements and the reassimilation of battle casualties who are returning to their units after a period in hospital requires care.** Young reinforcements in the 18 to 20 age group, who have not yet seen action, are a special problem in themselves. An effort to pair them up with older men who have battle experience and who can exercise a steadying influence may be better than allowing natural selection to pair weak with weak and strong with strong. Towards the end of a campaign, a number of psychiatric casualties may occur among men who have been wounded earlier in the campaign. Many will have sustained flesh wounds of no great severity but which have resulted in fairly lengthy stays in hospitals and convalescent depots. There has been abundant opportunity for brooding and the development of loss of confidence and a lowered morale. The feeling of invulnerability which is an accompaniment of high morale has been shattered by the wound ; the soldier feels different and certain that his luck has changed. The building up of the morale of the wounded man before return to duty ought not, therefore, to be neglected and attention concentrated purely on hardening the man physically.

When men feel that they are not sufficiently kept in the picture ; when they have little idea of what is going on or why, they are apt to become dispirited and to feel that they are regarded as cannon-fodder. They should be given the maximum information compatible with security. It is more necessary that men should appear to be in the confidence of their officers than that they should actually be given any very vital information which might endanger security.

The Environment

The adverse circumstances here are the very facts of war. In addition to battle stress, indirect mental and physical stresses such as loss of sleep, physical exhaustion, persistent and overwhelming noise, hunger, inability to retaliate at the enemy, etc., are often of great significance. Signs of breakdown become increasingly common in men who have undergone long campaign periods. Just as the average car wears out, so it appears that the soldier wears out, and when the duration of the campaign surpasses his limit then he will break down. Effective life as a combatant soldier depends largely on how continuously he is used in battle. This class of case—the worn out soldier—was seen in considerable numbers during the early part of the North West European campaign, when a number of men broke down who were experienced veterans with excellent past records.

CHAPTER 3

PSYCHOPATHOLOGY

Essentially the cause of the condition is fear. Battle stress and the accompanying fear may result in bodily changes, which are merely a normal and natural physiological reaction. Muscular tension increases, and a statement by a soldier such as " I get all keyed up and cannot relax " indicates an entirely normal reaction in the circumstances and one which may be accompanied by shaking, excessive sweating, urinary frequency, tachycardia, irritability, etc. It is normal also to become progressively more apprehensive before going into battle, to become increasingly sensitive to noise, etc. These are normal physiological reactions to fear and as such do not indicate that the individual is necessarily mentally incapable of further combat duty and so should be withdrawn from combat.

Fear in small quantity stimulates attention, sharpens judgement and evokes a maximal effort. Only when it dominates the mind is it harmful. Fear does not always walk naked and unashamed. In some it does, but in many it is disguised. The barriers of upbringing, self pride and sense of duty act as restraining forces. If the desire for self preservation is high and the strength of the restraining forces is low then fear will overflow and manifest itself. If both are high there will be conflict between these mental forces. If at any time a further cause for fear is added the barrier may no longer hold and fear will overflow. All these forces are variables. The instinct of self preservation will vary in different men. As no two men regard an equal stimulus as causing the same amount of physical pain, so will no two men fear the same situation equally. The strength of the barrier erected against the expression of fear will vary not only between men of different upbringing, education and values but in the same man at different times. It will be lowered by fatigue, pain, hunger and other stresses. Few factors can adversely affect a soldier's resistance to fear so certainly as worrying about affairs at home. In this way, the man who receives regular letters from his wife is placed at a great advantage over the man who has been overseas for some years and has to rely on irregular mail from home for reassuring news. A man who does not get along well with the others in his platoon is subjected to a similar non battle stress.

Primarily, there will be two types of psychiatric casualty :—the pure " fear " casualty and the pure " conflict " casualty. The former is the man with a low resistance to the instinct of self preservation by flight : the man in whom fear overflows the barrier and pours forth manifest. His symptoms will be those of fear, but his display of fear is disproportionate to the environment at the moment and the noise of distant shell fire may increase it. The onset may be slow and insidious and its recognition may demand keen observation in the early stages. Or it may come on acutely, and the man may be seen for the first time in a fully fledged state of panic. Some quite petty danger may be the last straw, which, added to the increasing self preservation forces, enables these forces to pour over the barrier and allow the suppressed fear of the past few weeks or months to follow. A state of fear may have been suppressed during the whole period in which it was engendered, only to display itself when all cause for fear has gone. When all cause for fear has gone, all means to resist fear, such as pride, sense of duty, may have also gone.

The pure " conflict " neurosis arises in the man who has both a high level of inclination to flight and a high level of other factors in his personality which resist the fulfilment of that inclination. He is, therefore, subjected to a conflict between these two mental forces with, in consequence, feelings of indecision, insecurity, uneasiness and tension. Under these conditions, a man who is usually quiet may become extremely talkative. This helps to liberate some of the pent up forces within him. Another man, usually talkative, may, become quiet because he is unable to maintain a sufficiently steady flow of thought to hold a conversation. Some may become so affected by the mental conflict that they will be almost stuporous. Others will be worried, disturbed by the tension and complain of insomnia. In more advanced cases, loss of memory may occur.

These two types of psychiatric casualty seldom occur in pure form. In most, fear and conflict are found together. Some men will break down quickly in their first severe action ; some will develop a slow breakdown which becomes worse with every action ; others will stand up well for months of a severe campaign, and a few who have stood up well to all actions will develop their symptoms in a quiet period. Reactions vary with personalities and circumstances ; some men become anxious more easily than others, and some can tolerate larger amounts of anxiety without breaking down than others.

CHAPTER 4

CLINICAL SYNDROMES

In the main, two psychiatric problems will confront the R.M.O., in the field : acute reactions arising during or shortly after battle, and chronic reactions which present themselves in a " quiet period ".

ACUTE PSYCHIATRIC CASUALTIES IN BATTLE

Clinical Types

1. EXHAUSTION

In a long battle when a unit has had little chance of sleep or rest, weary, apathetic, trembling, slow speaking men may present themselves in some numbers at the R.A.P. Many are men of good personality who have tolerated large quantities of anxiety in distressing circumstances for long periods but have eventually been called to a halt by the fatigue which unrelieved tension engenders. Physical exhaustion will add to the degree of fatigue, but exhaustion may occur in the absence of physical exertion. They are true psychiatric casualties and the exhaustion they show is a result of many hours of anxiety uninterrupted by good quality sleep. This type of case is usually seen after about the third day of a long battle and may exhibit other psychiatric symptoms as well as thi exhaustion state. They are easily recognized as suffering from gross fatigue, but the anxiety underlying the conditions must not be underestimated for it may prevent the man from sleeping even if given the opportunity in a quiet place. They are more common in long drawn out and severe battles than when the battle is short and sharp. Eventually the prolonged emotional tension produces a typical psychosomatic state.

Example

A private soldier on the fourth day of a battle in which enemy mortars had given much trouble, arrived at the R.A.P. showing obvious weariness and lassitude. He was trembling and " jumpy " at the sound of distant explosions, and apathetic and disinterested in the progress of the battle.

2. ANXIETY STATES

These constitute the commonest clinical syndrome met with in psychiatric casualties in battle. A small proportion of them are acute terror conditions of sudden onset which may affect immature youths in their first battle, or, less often, men of good previous personality who have been under conditions of great strain. The symptoms of this panic state vary and may take the form of either a positive or a negative reaction to the precipitating situation. The individual may shout and scream, run about aimlessly and show the typical signs of acute panic or he may appear dazed, confused or even semi-stuporous. The condition is transient ; the precipitating factors are usually obvious, and the response to suitable treatment is usually rapid.

In the majority of cases, the symptoms of the anxiety state may be mild with sweating, trembling, insomnia, battle dreams, startle reaction and anxious expectation of being hit. Outlook for return to duty after treatment is usually good. Less commonly they are more severe with uncontrollable startle reaction, coarse tremors of the limbs, and sudden fits of crying. These more severe cases seldom respond to any short period of treatment, but after more lengthy treatment at the base can be expected to recover sufficiently to return to duty in a lowered medical category in L. of C. or base areas.

Examples

A private soldier was blown up by a shell which killed his section corporal. He remained in action for another two hours under desultory shell fire but was jumpy and needed much persuasion to stay with his platoon. He took cover quickly at the slightest noise and was a nuisance to his officer who reported that his other men were being upset by this behaviour. At the R.A.P. he was trembling, showed marked startle reaction, restlessness and stammer and said that he was trying to control himself but could not. He was treated promptly, recovered within three days and was fighting well with his unit within a week.

After ten days in a dangerous situation from which evacuation was difficult, a private soldier became increasingly anxious, eventually running around screaming whenever enemy aircraft appeared. Between air raids he was trembling and sweating, always glancing at the sky and flinging himself down on the slightest sudden noise. At the R.A.P. he was seen to be a tense, terrified man and appeared to be listening for something. He was unable to bear any sudden noise, even a voice, without throwing himself on the ground.

Such gross free anxiety as in this last case may be quickly overshadowed by the mental mechanisms employed by mankind as a protection against the experience of prolonged, intense anxiety, *i.e.*, by hysterical conversion, confusion, phobias, acute psychosomatic illnesses and psychotic reactions. Within a few days, a grossly anxious man may show a combination of some of these protective mechanisms, and the ordinary signs of anxiety, *i.e.* tremor, startle reaction, etc., may thus be replaced to a greater or lesser degree by other symptoms.

3. STUPOROUS OR CONFUSIONAL STATES

In some men, prolonged severe anxiety leads to confusion of degrees varying from an inability to recall the day or exact circumstances of a battle to complete disorientation and resistive stupor. If stuporous, the man will ignore food and attention, resist attempts to help him, be apparently oblivious to what is going on around him and make no response to questions. The condition may closely simulate an acute schizophrenic reaction. The stuporous state usually lasts only a few hours but may persist for days or weeks. During convalescence, hysterical conversion symptoms frequently develop. The prognosis for return to full combatant duty after treatment is poor.

Example

A Captain of Infantry was admitted in a state of gross stupor, entirely mute and inaccessible. It was reported that his brother had been killed by a burst of shell before his eyes. With treatment his stupor disappeared and he was able to give a complete history. He began, however, to complain of pains behind the eyes and feared loss of vision.

4. HYSTERICAL REACTIONS

When anxiety is gross or prolonged, the man may protect himself from this by developing hysterical symptoms. These are self protective and render him incapable of further exposure to battle stress. The anxiety is covered up by the development of such hysterical symptoms as paralysis of various parts of the body, deafness, amblyopia, etc. The final state is then more tolerable than the first and it therefore follows that the rapid removal of these protective hysterical symptoms will inevitably lead to a recrudescence of the gross anxiety the man experienced before. This recrudescence of anxiety may be solved in turn by the development of a second and different set of hysterical symptoms.

Examples

A private soldier had been in action off and on for 65 days. A shell landed on the edge of his trench. He covered his face with his hands. When he removed them he was blind.

A private soldier had been in action off and on for 58 days and had had little rest. During an advance he encountered heavy shelling on open ground. There was no time to dig a trench and he was badly shaken. Enemy tanks were then silenced, and when he went to examine one he found a dying French boy who reminded him of his own son. He became speechless and was evacuated with aphonia and an uncontrollable jerking of the head and all limbs.

An officer aged 30 was admitted suffering from a paralysis of the left leg. His carrier had had a direct hit and he decided to crawl forward with his wireless and locate the enemy guns. A mortar bomb burst near him and his leg was bruised. He was also stunned and then evacuated. The manner in which he demonstrated the paralysis of his leg was pathognomonic. It improved and he was returned to his unit but was again evacuated in a few days in an acute state of reactive depression.

The hysterical overlay can, as a rule, be easily removed but the underlying anxiety state must subsequently be treated. Few respond well to treatment in forward areas because of the danger of a relapse with a fresh conversion symptom. The conversion symptom may sometimes have a deceptive basis of superficial logic, i.e., " I was knocked out and when I came to my leg was like this ". Hysterical conversion symptoms may cover many intolerably strong emotions such as mourning for the loss of comrades, unwarranted shame over a valiant failure, the home sickness of a brave soldier who has fought long and well and are not, therefore, necessarily merely a solution of a conflict between a sense of duty and a desire for self preservation. In some, the loss of function quickly yields to firm suggestion and persuasion if treated promptly. If treatment is delayed, however, all sorts of histrionic additional symptoms may be added. In others, the hysterical symptoms may only have developed after prolonged and severe strain in men of high morale and do not yield readily to simple, rapid methods of treatment.

Hysterical amnesias and fugues may occur as a protection from an amount of free anxiety which is unbearably great. When anxiety is prolonged and gross the soldier may pass into a highly receptive emotional state. Experiences such as a " near miss " may then result in his believing that he is shortly to be killed and a massive protective response in the form of a complete loss of memory may be evoked. He may lie mute and still or may wander off and be picked up some distance from his unit, being then either fully conscious but unable to remember anything before his fugue or fully recovered from his fugue but unable to account for his movements during it. Medico-legal problems may complicate the issue. The more rapidly he is abreacted and reintegrated the better. Such cases are not common, but minor amnesias for battle incidents are a relatively common phenomenon, and the extent claimed is often in excess of the truth. In many, the claim of amnesia requires careful scrutiny. Whatever form of treatment is given, i.e., vigorous persuasion with or without abreactive treatment, etc., it must be carried out promptly and efficiently. Failure to do so may result in the addition of other more gross hysterical manifestations.

Examples

A private soldier who had never been in action was sitting in a L. of C. area watching a flight of planes. He remembered no more until he came to bending over a ditch and trying to wash blood stains from his tunic. He had a complete amnesia. With treatment, he recovered his memory and said that when his comrade and himself were looking at the planes they dived down. His comrade slumped forward and when he went to his assistance and tried to remove his helmet the head came away with the helmet. He dashed blindly from the spot.

Following a direct hit on his command post, an officer developed a severe retrograde amnesia. Evacuated to hospital where he was unable to provide even his name. With treatment he quickly recovered his memory but developed fainting attacks whenever he was asked to relate his battle experiences.

5. PSYCHOSOMATIC DISORDERS

Exhaustion is the commonest disabling somatic result of unrelieved anxiety on the battle field and has been dealt with under a different heading. Other physical symptoms expressing anxiety and likely to be met with singly or in combination are headache, stammering, incontinence, tics, vomiting, indigestion, etc. These psychosomatic disorders are liable to become chronic, and if their underlying emotional genesis is not recognized they may eventually be diagnosed as purely physical conditions. In the acute phase, they are almost invariably accompanied by some free anxiety which makes diagnosis easier. They are not a major problem during battle but if not recognized and correctly handled they will often herald chronic illness.

6. DEPRESSION

Depression may dominate the picture, and is a typical reaction to battle stress which ought to be recognized. This depression seems to be similar to the normal mourning reaction that follows the death of a beloved relative, and in war is seen most often in soldiers who have lost their comrades or a particularly well liked officer in battle, or have been exposed to unsavoury experiences. Strong unconscious guilt feelings may play a part in the psychopathology of the condition, and, therefore, it may be helpful if soldiers can sometimes be given the opportunity to mourn the loss of comrades. Memorial services after battle may serve a useful prophylactic purpose in discharging unconscious guilt. An over-sympathetic or over-tough method of approach does harm in cases of depression. They require objective understanding with active practical measures to help them. The risk of suicide must be remembered.

7. PSYCHOSIS

Under the stress of unbearable experiences, acute psychotic reactions may be seen. They are, however, not common. During great stress, anxiety may be quickly shelved by the development of a withdrawal into psychosis with symptom complexes such as resistive catatonic stupor, hallucinations and bizarre kinds of behaviour. A form of schizophrenic syndrome may be presented. These psychotic mechanisms arise in pre-disposed personality types as a protection from massive anxiety. The prognosis is generally good.

8. MIXED TYPES

The above seven reactions are not always seen in pure culture. Many, when first seen, present a few features of each mechanism, while others may, in the course of a week, show a succession of several distinct reactions, all with the same function—the protection of the individual from free anxiety.

9. MINOR SYMPTOMS

The mild and understandable anxiety shown by almost all men who have been through a severe battle, their jumpiness, anxiety, dreams, etc., may, if a man's morale is poor, affect his behaviour. He may then cease to be an efficient soldier and report sick with trembling, sweating, an anxious expectation of being hit and a complaint of being " unable to stand it any longer ". This is a common group, and symptoms usually disappear as soon as the man is out of sound of the guns. Treatment should be immediate and far forward and should result in a return to duty of the very great majority.

Comparative incidence

The incidence of free anxiety depends on the degree of stress, and that of exhaustion mainly on the duration of the stress: The types and numbers of cases seen will, therefore, vary with the kind of battle which is experienced. **In the average battle of moderate duration and intensity, about one third of the cases seen in the forward areas will be those of mild free anxiety, another third will be cases of exhaustion, some showing mild anxiety and minor hysterical tremors, and the remaining third will be comprised of cases of hysterical and mixed reactions, confusions and depressions.**

Prognosis

Taken as a whole, the prognosis for early return to duty of psychiatric casualties is better than that of any other type of battle casualty. Only the mildest, however, will recover spontaneously. On the other hand, many mild cases will recover if given half a chance, and psychiatric first aid at the R.A.P. may be all that they require. Cases which will respond best to such simple methods of treatment as are available at the R.A.P. are mild cases of exhaustion and of free anxiety. A simple hysterical conversion state such as dimness of vision may exceptionally be treated by the R.M.O. at the R.A.P. If this can be done it may be an excellent form of treatment, but it is realized that circumstances at the R.A.P. especially during battle will rarely make it possible. Most hysterical conversion states, and almost all depressions, confusions and severe anxiety states will respond better if evacuated from the R.A.P. Of those so evacuated, most cases of exhaustion, moderate cases of free anxiety and mild cases of hysteria and confusion should return within a short time fit for further combat duty with their own unit. The prognosis for the other clinical types is not good for further front line duties. The ultimate prognosis for service in L. of C. and base areas is, however, good for most of the grosser clinical types, and arrangements for the specific re-employment of partially recovered psychiatric casualties should exist in the rear areas. Only the worst or badly mishandled cases will not improve to the degree of being useful in some capacity and so require to be evacuated from the theatre. The prognosis for the majority is better if they can be treated " just behind the noise ". The sound of distant gun fire does not worry them unduly. If evacuation from the unit is necessary, then the quicker the case is evacuated and treated, preferably in the divisional area, and promptly returned to duty after treatment, the better are the chances of recovery as a fighting man. The psychiatric casualty who is evacuated beyond the corps area is often forever lost to his unit. Symptoms become fixed and difficult to eradicate the longer treatment is delayed and the further the case is evacuated from the front. Simple measures no longer then suffice and skilled and lengthy specialist treatment may be necessary. **Approximately 50 to 60 per cent. of all psychiatric casualties in battle evacuated from their units and treated in a divisional centre may be expected to become fit for further combat duty in their own units within a period of 7 days. Of the remaining 40 to 50 per cent., a varying percentage will become fit for further combat duty after about 10 to 14 days' treatment in a corps centre.** The majority, however, of those who do not respond to treatment in, and are evacuated from, a divisional centre will, after treatment in a corps or base centre, be fit for further duty only in a restricted capacity, *i.e.*, in L. of C. or base areas.

Chronic Reactions

During the course of a long campaign, certain chronic changes of attitude are the inevitable result of the strain of war and the cumulative stresses of battle. The digestion of experiences in battle, the deaths of friends, separation from home and the few facilities for full relaxation all form a mounting framework upon which develop certain common psychological reactions. Just as the common emotion which results from battle is anxiety, so the common emotion here is depression. This may be mild or severe and may contain certain elements of the primary anxiety from which it is fashioned. It can be handled by the sufferer in various ways and the different mental mechanisms used for off-setting this basic depression may give rise to certain recognizable disturbances of attitude. The common chronic reactions are :—

Depression

A soldier may become quiet, keep more than usual by himself, become unable to mix with the same zest as before, show an unwonted degree of humourless, quiet and apathetic inactivity, and cease to take an interest in unit games or spare time pursuits. He may smoke too much or drink too much. Such a state may be precipitated by bad news from home or lack of mail but may also develop without any such obvious precipitating stimulus. The condition may remain in this mild form, but the soldier's value to his unit is already impaired. If he gets worse, he may have difficulty in sleeping, have anxiety dreams and may on occasion weep when by himself. His value in battle may become minimal. This form of reaction respects nobody and may occur particularly in a conscientious man with a high sense of duty. He will not often complain directly to his medical officer until in a state of undisguised depression, although he may approach him earlier with a minor complaint, i.e., insomnia, and hope thereby that the medical officer will notice the depression which he is too ashamed to mentioned himself.

Paranoid Escape

Some men in an endeavour to throw off their gloom and the sense of being forsaken, project their feelings so that when they feel badly they look for evidence of evil or distrust in those around them. They become resentful of details of official discipline, chronically disgruntled, cynical and bitter. They may develop suspicions, sometimes on the flimsiest evidence, that their wives are unfaithful. This reaction may reach a stage when the individual becomes a nuisance to his unit and a danger to his comrades' morale. When this stage arises in an officer, the morale of his subordinates will be affected by his irritability and bitterness, and it may become a serious threat to unit morale.

Psychosomatic expression

The depression and anxiety may find expression in certain autonomic disturbances. Loss of physical energy, mild headaches, liability to certain skin disorders and eye trouble, insomnia, anorexia, memory difficulties and secondary hysterical fixation of minor injuries and complaints are fairly common signs of an underlying chronic mild depression. They are met mostly in men who have been in action fairly continuously for long periods.

Mixed Reactions

The various mechanisms by which depression is handled may exist side by side with residual anxieties from recent battles which show themselves by nightmares, minor phobias, etc.

These chronic reactions to war are sometimes isolated and individual, and are then clinical problems requiring the ordinary doctor-patient relationship for their solution. At other times, instances of infectious minor disturbances of this nature may become so common within a unit that a group problem presents itself. A group attitude, however, is unlikely to deteriorate badly when unit welfare is good and when men can feel that, no matter what experiences they have undergone, their officers are active in their interest, energetic in sharing and minimizing their discomforts and hold them in high comradely esteem. Feelings of psychological security and worth are the mainsprings of the positive mental health that permits long campaigning and exposure to fear without breakdown.

CHAPTER 5

PREVENTION

In psychiatry, as elsewhere, prevention is better than cure, and in no field is this more likely to produce effective results than in psychiatric breakdown in battle. Prevention to be effective, however, depends on an adequate understanding of the cause. Much can be done by measures taken well before the entry of troops into battle. Adequate selection and screening out of those most heavily predisposed to breakdown will pay good dividends. Such men can be picked out with certainty during psychiatric interview. Selection by elimination is not, however, the solution to the problem of prevention. **It is impossible to eliminate in advance all men who are likely to breakdown in battle, no matter how thorough the process of screening. The way in which men are treated and the manner in which they are led are also factors of vital importance. If motivation, morale and leadership are good, certain men with a predisposition to breakdown will endure severe battle stress.**

It is important also for all men to realize that fear is a natural reaction to the circumstances of combat and is felt by all normal men—a simple fact which is overlooked by some. To feel fear is not something to be ashamed of, and is quite different from cowardice. The man who is ashamed of feeling fear is a man who is more likely to mishandle his own emotional difficulties in battle and so more prone to breakdown. It is a normal battle risk and ought to be understood, faced and overcome. There is no chance of suppressing fear merely by forbidding discussion about it. This normal battle reaction of fear may produce symptoms which are merely the normal autonomic response to fear. Though such symptoms might be classified as abnormal in a civilian setting, they are normal in a battle setting and must be regarded as such by the medical officer. **Any mismanagement by the R.M.O. during battle, such as unnecessary evacuation, may lead to the development of abnormal neurotic reactions with a view to perpetuating the gain which has resulted from evacuation.** Though evacuation of such a case is a wrong method of disposal, this should not imply that the soldier reporting to the R.M.O. with symptoms of a normal battle fear reaction should be summarily returned to duty. He must return to duty but should first be given an explanation of his symptoms in simple terms. He should be told that his complaints represent a normal response to fear which are also experienced by many of his comrades in the line, and he should be reassured and encouraged. The R.M.O. who really knows his unit will also be able to pick out during rest periods men who are showing incipient signs of breakdown. A friendly talk, a mild sedative such as phenobarbitone, or perhaps a night in the R.A.P. with proper sedation may often be sufficient. The R.M.O. has a special responsibility to the willing horse—the man, usually a warrant officer or N.C.O., who has been one of the mainstays of his unit but is showing signs of a deterioration in his spirits and efficiency. Such a man, if he finally breaks down, often does so badly and is rarely able to return after any short period of treatment.

Apart from combat stress, indirect physical stresses such as loss of sleep, physical exhaustion, etc., play a considerable part, and some breakdowns may be prevented by an occasional enforced rest. It may be possible to have some sort of rest centre near unit H.Q. to which men can be sent when showing signs of strain.

The problem of prevention is one, however, which affects all officers, and not primarily those of the medical services alone. If the leader passes on his intentions and the plans by which he intends to carry them out ; if each man believes in his leader and his cause ; if physical and mental fitness together with technical skill have been brought to a high level, and if the factors mentioned in the causation have been given earnest attention, then the incidence of mental breakdown among troops will be low.

Special attention should be given to reinforcements. Battle inexperienced troops are subject to appreciably higher breakdown rates. Methods such as that of battle inoculation in battle schools will help but much more will be effected by carefully introducing units and reinforcements to combat.

Lying behind all considerations is good leadership, which is the most important single factor in prevention. The number of psychiatric battle casualties in any unit is an indication of the state of morale and efficiency of that unit. They are often a reflection on the leaders rather than on the led. In spite, however, of all efforts to achieve prevention it will be too much to expect that breakdown will be entirely absent, for even a mechanized army is ultimately composed of human material.

It is, therefore, important that every effort should be made to treat them with intelligent understanding when they occur. The beliefs that no man should break down in battle and certainly no one should be " allowed " to break down are not particularly helpful.

CHAPTER 6

TREATMENT

AT UNIT LEVEL

Every medical officer in a division should have a sound working knowledge of the recognition and treatment of psychiatric casualties in battle. The good R.M.O. can be of prime importance in their prevention, and, when they occur, much depends on his ability to handle them correctly in the early stages before the abnormal reactions become stabilized and fixed. Early treatment should begin, and, in some cases, end with the R.M.O., who can do much towards sustaining the morale of his unit by a correct method of disposal. If he is too lenient and indiscriminately evacuates mild cases and men who are exhibiting only normal physiological reactions to battle stress and are mentally capable of carrying on, then he may help towards undermining the determination of others to fight on. They, too, may begin to think that they are sick and deserving of evacuation. On the other hand, if he is too strict and harsh and returns men to duty who are mentally incapable of carrying on effectively, then he removes the confidence the personnel of a unit should have in their medical officer, which also is detrimental to unit morale in battle. **It is highly important to avoid indiscrimate evacuation of psychiatric casualties.** A few such unnecessary evacuations may be likened to the falling stone which can start an avalanche. If treatment on the spot is possible and is carried out, then progress is as a rule much better.

In the stress of battle, the most vital question is not how to remove certain symptoms. The battle field is no place for experiments in accurate diagnosis. Much wider considerations must be faced : Is the soldier fit to remain in the line ? Can I make him fit by treatment within the unit ? If evacuation from the unit is necessary, what first aid treatment must I give ? What will be the effect of this evacuation on those who remain ? The R.M.O. should be guided not only by the type and degree of the psychiatric disability but also by the unit's military needs at the moment ; whether the man is still of some immediate use ; how long the battle has been going on ; the level of unit morale and the interests of the individual man. He may have to be hard but the battle area is a hard place. Only, however, if he has faced up squarely to his own fears will he attain a real professional detachment and avoid the extremes of ineffective harshness and excessive sympathy. **No soldier capable of fighting should be able to regard the R.A.P. as an honourable avenue of retreat from the battle field.** The presence or absence of symptoms of anxiety is not the main consideration here. In combat, most soldiers have anxiety and show some of the psycho-somatic symptoms of anxiety. The important consideration in combat is whether or not the anxiety present is of such severity that the soldier is incapacitated for combat. This, rather than the presence of anxiety, should be the criterion for evacuation from a R.A.P. A number of psychiatric casualties reporting to the R.A.P. during battle can be likened to an outbreak of some infectious disease, and should authorize the R.M.O. to investigate the cause and recommend measures to limit its spread.

As soon as it becomes known that a unit is about to take part in an operation, a mixed group of men may report sick. Some may be chronic neurotics who should have been weeded out earlier ; others will be insecure, hysterical personalities, and a few are cases of true anxiety in men who can be assumed to be anxiety prone. A very small group is represented by a good type of man who is perhaps overstrained and is simply manifesting a physiological response comparable to that of the boxer about to enter a ring.

If symptoms arise in battle, the decision whether or not the case should be sent to the R.M.O. will have to be made by the company commander. Every effort ought to be made by the latter to keep the merely frightened soldier in action. Young lads of 18 to 20 breaking down in their first action often represent a morale problem related to lack of absorption and identification with the unit. They are a special problem by themselves. A good platoon commander may help by taking them apart as a group before their first action and discussing in simple terms what they are likely to meet with, how they are likely to feel and what to do about it. In this way they will not only be given more confidence but will feel that their performance is something that really matters to their unit. With young untried reinforcements an effort might be made to pair them up with older men who can exercise a steadying influence rather than to allow natural selection to pair weak with weak. The appointment of two more stolid and preferably seasoned soldiers to whom the weaker comrade can be entrusted for a forthcoming action may be tried. It should be the duty of these two " battle friends " to keep as close to their charge as dispersal requirements permit and at all times to help and encourage him. All three should understand the relationship and the two " battle friends " should be carefully chosen.

If the unit officer decides to send the soldier to the R.M.O. during battle, written authority must, if at all possible, be given by the officer for the casualty to be evacuated to the R.A.P. No psychiatric casualty should be allowed to leave the battle field without written permission. It is also particularly useful to those medical officers who may subsequently have to treat the case to know whether the claims, often extravagant, which may later be made by the casualty are true in fact. A note from the combatant officer about the circumstances leading up to the man's evacuation to the R.A.P. may, therefore, be of great assistance later in the assessment of the case.

The R.M.O. will have to decide for or against evacuation from the unit. Gross forms of psychiatric casualties should present few difficulties in diagnosis and disposal. Certain cases, however, call for discrimination and mature judgement. The following are some examples :—

   (a) The young soldier unduly frightened in his first battle.
   (b) The frightened man who has been badly led or whose officer has become a casualty.
   (c) The man who gives a doubtful history of having lost consciousness for a few minutes after a shell burst.
   (d) The man who reports at the R.A.P. without written authority from his officer.

To some extent the decision for or against evacuation will be governed by the tactical situation. If the R.A.P. is sufficiently static, dramatic results can be obtained in mild cases by a meal, sweet hot drinks, and sleep assisted by a sedative. A generous dose should be given. Mild cases may require 6 to 12 hours' sleep only, but this should be of good quality. A unit's B Echelon may sometimes be used for this short rest, but much will depend on local conditions. Usually B Echelon is no place for acute psychiatric cases and earlier return of an efficient man to his unit is often more likely to follow evacuation in the first place to a divisional exhaustion centre if treatment is impossible at the R.A.P. After 6 to 12 hours of sedated sleep at the R.A.P., the majority of mild cases will be more stable and ready, after a short interview with the R.M.O., to return to duty. The R.M.O. does not require any special or elaborate technique. A brief enquiry into the symptomatology, an explanation of the condition in simple terms and reassurance will often suffice. Much depends on the reputation of the R.M.O. If he has been consistent and firm but fair in his handling of these casualties his results will be good, and the patient will generally be willing to accept the opinion that he is fit to return. Leading in these cases is usually better than pushing. The R.M.O., however, will be unable to treat more than a certain number at his R.A.P., and therapeutic optimism resulting in the return of an unreliable man to his officer is no help to a unit engaged in battle. **Urgency of treatment is all important, and normally no case should be retained at the R.A.P. during battle which requires more than one generous dose of sedative or more than 24 hours' treatment at the R.A.P.** Men who are evacuated from the R.A.P. should be given the impression that they will, after a short period of treatment elsewhere, be returning once again to their units.

Selection of cases suitable for retention at the R.A.P. is more complex in theory than in practice. In general, only the mildest should be retained, although there may be periods when even the severest cannot be evacuated or when even mild cases cannot be held. A sound disposal judgement of genuine psychiatric casualties can usually be made on the answers to the questions : " How much use is the man to his unit in the line now and in his present state ? " and " Can I make him a useful soldier by treating him in the R.A.P. for 24 hours ? " Needless evacuation on the one hand, and the holding of cases at the R.A.P. until the prognosis is hopeless on the other hand, can both be avoided by bearing these two questions in mind. The question will sometimes arise whether an individual soldier who is behaving in a timorous way should be treated as a sick man or by disciplinary means. This question, always vexed in theory, is seldom difficult in an actual case. It should be decided by the R.M.O. on practical common sense grounds. **Medical channels of evacuation should not be abused to rid the unit of men who are ineffective in battle because of unwillingness rather than inability to carry on.** Such men may be referred to the R.M.O. by their unit officer in the hope that a psychiatric diagnosis may be made and open up a convenient and easy method of disposal. **If a soldier is mentally capable of carrying on, there should, in battle, be no evacuation through medical channels.** The need for early treatment of true psychiatric casualties must not lead to any misunderstanding in the soldier's mind and be an encouragement to him to report sick early. Normal physiological reactions must be endured in battle. The R.M.O. should try and explain to a soldier reporting with such normal reactions how the symptoms have arisen and how they do not differ greatly from those experienced by most other men in the line. No complete relief is possible. They must be endured. Should, however, this type of case be evacuated, then the evacuation helps to confirm the man's belief that his condition is serious. Unconsciously, or otherwise, he discovers that his illness is an asset. His symptoms become fixed or perhaps increase in order to perpetuate the gain they produce. The few who deliberately avoid action, who wander away symptom-free and who subsequently report at the R.A.P. should be returned to duty. It is, however, no part of the R.M.O's. duty to decide whether or not a soldier should have disciplinary action taken against him. In times of stress one cannot afford to be lenient towards men who withdraw from combat with fear and state simply that they will not go back, and have no true psychiatric disability entitling them to evacuation. If treated leniently and with undue consideration they invite imitation by others.

In his handling of psychiatric casualties the R.M.O. must be absolutely honest. He should exhibit a mixture of firmness, sympathy and friendly encouragement. An understanding but not too lenient helping hand may help many to finish the battle.

Without interest and tolerance the R.M.O. is defeated but sentimentality and anger play no part. These only adversely affect true clinical judgement and correct disposal.

The case of the officer or senior N.C.O. may demand special consideration. Because of their responsibilities to others, it may often be wiser to evacuate an officer or senior N.C.O. when instability becomes evident.

A common fear is that evacuation of psychiatric casualties from a unit may lead to a " backward looking " mentality in the unit. A psychiatric casualty, however, is usually a nuisance in his unit and a menace to the safety and morale of his comrades. Fear is infectious and anxious individuals are no assets to their comrades who have enough to do controlling their own emotions and getting on with the battle. Since the policy of the divisional and corps exhaustion centres is to return to the unit within a week in the case of divisional centres and within 14 days in the case of corps centres every case possible, and approximately 60 to 70 per cent. will be so returned, a general policy of wholesale evacuation from the forward areas to base will never in fact be in force. If it is not possible to treat certain cases at the R A P. then early evacuation to the divisional centre, effective treatment there and quick return to the unit will keep more men in action than late evacuation of hopeless cases and consequent permanent loss to their units.

All psychiatric cases evacuated from the R.A.P. during battle should be marked " Exhaustion " on the Field Medical Card, and should generally be evacuated under sedation with the dose and time of administration noted on the Field Medical Card. This term " Exhaustion " should be used only for battle cases. It is a convenient administrative rather than a medical diagnosis. It is important that the soldier who is suffering from a condition which is good in its immediate prognosis should have a diagnosis given him which if he reads it—and he almost certainly will—will have suggested to him that it is a temporary condition. To make an accurate differential diagnosis between physical exhaustion and psychiatric illness or mixtures thereof is impossible for the busy R.M.O. in battle in the absence of psychiatric training. The " exhaustion " casualty should be entered as " sick " and not as battle casualty in the Field Medical Card. Those who are anxious, apprehensive and agitated may be given barbitone soluble gr. X-XV. Full narcosis should be used only when the case is very noisy and restless. Maintenance doses of sedative may be required in medical units on the line of evacuation.

During quiet rest periods the R.M.O. should look for early symptoms of breakdown ; some form of psychiatric first aid and prophylactic first aid may then be invaluable. During this period the R.M.O. should arrange, in co-operation with the divisional or corps psychiatrist, for the unit to be relieved of men who are inefficient because of gross dullness or extreme degrees of instability. During battle, evacuation must be limited to those who are incapacitated with illness. A considerable number of men may report sick with psychosomatic complaints during rest periods. A complete history and a thorough physical examination must first be carried out. The R.M.O. should then explain in simple terms how the symptoms have arisen. Provided the initial history taking and physical examination have been thorough, the soldier is often willing to admit an emotional basis for his symptoms. Referral for psychiatric and other specialist investigation should seldom be necessary, and the R.M.O. should familiarize himself with methods of explaining the emotional nature of symptom formation.

The psychiatric casualty who has been evacuated and has again returned to his unit after treatment in a divisional or corps centre requires careful handling. The welcome such men get in their units is the final part of their treatment, and early reintegration in the unit will do much to help the man regain his sense of security. It is important for the maintenance of his *esprit de corps* that he should be fitted whenever possible into his original place in his own unit and among his old comrades. He thus gets a reasonable chance to settle down quickly and feel at home before his comrades have forgotten him and closed their ranks. Some combatant officers may be reluctant to take back a man who has once been a psychiatric casualty, but the R.M.O. should insist that a new working assessment of the returned casualty be made and pre-judgement avoided.

Sedative Drugs

The drugs mentioned below are those useful for a man of average weight, but when there is much deviation from the average, proportionately more or less may be used. The drugs are given in order of their relative importance in the treatment of anxiety.

Treatment at the R.A.P.

For prophylactic use and for the treatment of mild cases at the R.A.P. moderate doses are indicated as follows :—

	Prophylactic	*Therapeutic*
Sodium amytal	gr. 3	gr. 6
Barbitone Soluble ..	gr. 5	gr. 10
Pentobarbitone soluble	gr. 1½	gr. 3
Phenobarbitone.. ..	gr. 2	gr. 3

Evacuation under sedation

Early sedation and its continuance throughout evacuation may prevent certain symptoms from becoming fixed. The dose given, however, must not be so large as to convert a walking into a stretcher case. The following is a useful dose range :—

Sodium amytal	gr. 6 to 9
Barbitone soluble ..	gr. 10 to 15
Pentobarbitone soluble	gr. 3
Phenobarbitone	gr. 3

Additional sedation during evacuation may be required for certain men after 6 hours, and medical units on the line of evacuation should be prepared, if necessary, to supplement the sedative given at the R.A.P. by a further dose decided by the clinical state of the patient. Enough should be given to maintain a state of quietude without gross ataxia. The dose and the time and date of all supplementary sedatives should be added to the details on the Field Medical Card.

The above drugs may not always be available and the following are good substitutes :—

Paraldehyde	Drachms 2
Phenobarbitone soluble (for intra muscular injection) ..	0.22 gm. Ampoule 1
Chloral hydrate	gr. 20
Sodium bromide	gr. 40

TREATMENT AT DIVISIONAL LEVEL

In World War II, the organization for dealing with psychiatric casualties in forward areas gradually evolved as a result of practical experience, and towards the end of the war a psychiatrist was, whenever practicable, attached to each actively fighting division. Failing this, the corps psychiatrist attempted to set up a treatment centre staffed by specially trained medical officers in each division. Experience showed that the presence of more than academic qualifications in psychiatry was necessary in the selection of a divisional psychiatrist. He required to be not only a good psychiatrist but also a good medical officer. Previous experience in a field unit was essential as was also a good knowledge and understanding of the problems and difficulties of the soldier.

The advantages of having treatment centres in divisions were considerable. Men treated there were still within the " family ", and intimate contact was possible between the centre and the R.M.Os. of the division. The " gain from illness " syndrome which often follows evacuation further back was less and subsequent fixation of a man's symptoms did not occur to the same extent. The medical unit which was principally used for the forward treatment of psychiatric casualties was the Field Dressing Station. Psychiatric casualties in battle tend to come in rushes of greater or less intensity according to the severity or prolongation of the battle, and such factors as victory or defeat, greenness or hardness of the troops engaged, etc. Combat inexperienced divisions engaged for the first time in major battles often produced a considerable crop of such casualties until the division " shook down ". Any scheme, therefore, for dealing with the forward treatment of psychiatric casualties must be an elastic one. The sudden rise in casualtieswhich may occur after a new division goes into its first action or when extreme stress and strain of battle are encountered may lead to hasty and ill-considered improvisations for dealing with the situation unless a competent psychiatric organization exists. The latter will return to duty a far higher proportion of cases than the former.

The work of a divisional psychiatrist may be considered from three aspects.

1. *Before battle and during rest periods*

The psychiatrist should make personal contact with the R.M.Os. in the area he serves and instruct them in the simpler methods of dealing with the re-adjustment of mild cases within the unit framework. The psychiatrist is greatly helped here if he knows something of the working conditions of a R.A.P. during action, and has experienced himself, in some small degree, the stresses of combat. A knowledge of individual R.M.Os. is of value, also, when considering the ultimate disposal of cases, implying, as it does, a knowledge of the standards on which evacuation has been determined by each R.M.O. The necessity of watching for early signs should be stressed, as also should the value of a " stitch in time ", and the unobtrusive weeding out from units of doubtful inadequates during rest periods. It is particularly important for the R.M.O. to check over new unit reinforcements. **It is useful also if a series of lectures or informal talks can be given to the combatant officers who are in direct contact with soldiers.** The latter should realize the importance of leadership in preventing this type of casualty, should have an understanding of the normal man's reaction to combat and the abnormal reaction shown by genuine psychiatric casualties, and should be able to do a certain amount of psychiatric first aid. All should realize the importance of prevention and that these casualties often indicate a failure of the leader rather than the led. The divisional psychiatrist should, however, be careful not to leave any impression in the minds of his listeners that psychiatric casualties can be wholly prevented and that no man should be allowed to break down. This may lead to the retention within a unit of men who are casualties in the true sense of the word and whose retention may be a menace to the morale of their comrades and a potential source of panic.

2. *During battle*

The ideal location for a divisional treatment centre is probably just " behind the noise ", and this might be in the divisional

maintenance area. The first and essential requirement for these
casualties at this stage is rest and sleep. The effects of shelling are
harmful ; mild cases become more severe, they rush to slit trenches
or may panic and infect others who have improved and are
endeavouring to regain their confidence and return to their units.
Heavy sedation will, of course, " drown " the noise, but heavy
sedation at this level is contra-indicated and indeed may be an
obstacle in the way of the quick return to duty which is an essential
basis of treatment at this level.

**The treatment given is a matter of individual choice but
only simple restorative and psychotherapeutic measures are
justified, and only men who are likely to respond to such
simple methods and are likely to be returned fit to their
units within a period of 7 days should be retained for treatment.** The psychiatrist should be kept well in the battle picture
and, therefore, in a position to judge, apart from the patient's own
statements, the physical and mental stresses to which he had been
subjected. Immediately after the essential needs of the case are
fulfilled on first arrival at the centre, a quick and largely intuitive
psychiatric appraisal must be made to decide whether the man will
be fit to fight after the limited period possible for treatment in the
centre. If not, the case should be evacuated to the corps exhaustion
centre. All psychotics, mental defectives, most relapses and severe
anxiety cases should be evacuated to the corps centre. The less
severe anxiety states in whom physical exhaustion has played a
part and the mild hysterics respond fairly well to treatment in the
divisional centre. It is important, also, initially to determine
whether the case is one primarily of physical exhaustion or whether
emotional causes were mainly responsible. The dose of sedative
required differs considerably in these two groups. During this initial
screening the psychiatrist must be on his guard for a possible
infective aetiology. This is particularly important in the tropics
where physical investigations not infrequently reveal toxic infective
conditions among cases of alleged mental disease. The fullest
physical examination may therefore be required and a thermometer
may be a vital article of the psychiatrist's equipment. In some cases
the degree of response to early therapy may have to be the guiding
factor in determining whether or not a man should be retained or
evacuated. If it is decided to evacuate a man to a corps centre,
he should merely be told that he is being transferred for treatment
at another centre. He should be given no indication that his case
is regarded as difficult or likely to require prolonged treatment.
If he is led directly or indirectly to believe this, then a major
obstacle has been placed in the way of any quick return to first
line duty.

If it is decided to retain the case for treatment at the divisional
centre, he should be given a hot meal followed by a long and if

possible uninterrupted sleep of 12 to 24 hours' duration. For some, no sedative may be required. To others, an initial dose of sodium amytal 3 to 6 grains may be given followed, if necessary, by an additional dose of 3 grains every six hours. Paraldehyde in doses of from 2 to 4 drachms is a safe and good substitute for sodium amytal and may be repeated in 2 drachm doses every six hours. Sodium pentothal may be useful to control acute, noisy and restless cases.

After a good sleep, a shower bath, shave, change of underclothing and a general tidy up should be made possible, and any minor organic disabilities present should receive attention. The best time for a psychiatric interview is probably 48 hours after admission to the centre. Tension and fear should now have eased, and the case should then be in a more receptive frame of mind to see the psychiatrist. The psychiatrist must of necessity restrict himself to the more superficial methods of therapy, *i.e.*, explanation, reassurance and encouragement. The more dramatic methods of treatment by prolonged narcosis, and abreaction should seldom be attempted. They are often only the first stages in a somewhat prolonged treatment. Patients should have their symptoms explained in simple terms. If the psychiatrist considers that the patient will be fit to return to duty from the centre, he should inform him so and that he will have a few days rest first. The patient must be left in no doubt, however, that on the termination of this period of rest he will return to his unit. **Men who wish to argue and claim that they are unfit to return to duty should never be told that their case will be finally decided after the few days' rest, and that, if not by then improved, evacuation may be considered. This approach must never be used.** The psychiatrist must make up his mind and make a decision and stick to it.

The remaining 4 to 5 days in the divisional centre should be regarded as a period of rehabilitation. A curative atmosphere should prevail and all must realize that the final disposal is a return to duty in the line. There should be a gradual but definite re-imposition of military discipline in the centre. Personal worries should be investigated ; facilities should be available for writing home, etc.; physical training and group talks given, and arrangements made for games and simple amusements. A final psychiatric interview should be given before discharge to duty, and a short report sent to the R.M.O. of the patient's unit.

Successful rehabilitation of psychiatric casualties depends also to a considerable extent on a correct attitude being maintained towards the patients by the medical orderlies in the centre. They respond like children to considerate treatment. As far as possible the lay out of the divisional centre should be on the lines indicated for a corps exhaustion centre.

TREATMENT AT CORPS LEVEL

The establishment of a corps exhaustion centre might be questioned when well organised divisional centres are functioning. The corps centre, however, provides a forward treatment centre for psychiatric casualties from overcrowded divisional centres or divisional centres which are moving. It provides, also, a more suitable site for the treatment of patients who react badly to the possibly noisy environment of the divisional centre, and enables further screening of cases to take place and ensures, therefore, that the maximum number of psychiatric casualties will be treated far forward. The best corps medical unit to use for this purpose cannot be answered dogmatically. Much will depend on geographical factors, the facilities for evacuation and the total beds available, etc. Accommodation in a C.C.S. may provide a convenient centre, but, unfortunately, the biggest rush of psychiatric casualties usually comes at times when there is a torrent of surgical cases. If the psychiatric centre is then located in a C.C.S. evacuation of all cases might be enforced, thus nullifying the corps psychiatrist's function in treatment. The use of a Field Dressing Station as an exhaustion centre was found generally satisfactory, but whatever or wherever the unit is established at least 50 beds, rising to 100 in an occasional emergency, should be available. The unit selected for the centre should be located as near C.C.S. level as possible.

Before the commencement of active operations, the corps psychiatrist should, by visits and lectures to the medical units in his area, explain the policy standards and disposal procedures. Informal talks stressing the importance of prophylaxis should be given to R.M.Os. and combatant officers. It may not always be possible to appoint psychiatrists to divisions ; if not, then the corps psychiatrist may be responsible for the training of medical officers to staff divisional exhaustion centres, and for keeping in close touch with them and supervising and assisting them in their work. **By keeping adequate records of the incidence of psychiatric casualties and by their incidence as compared with that of total battle casualties, the corps psychiatrist will be able to provide information about the morale of forward troops and the adequacy of the forward screening of psychiatric casualties.** After a battle, the corps psychiatrist should suggest to the D.D.M.S. Corps any changes of procedure which may appear to be desirable, and should assist in the combing out of unsuitable men from forward units.

During action, he should, if possible, be so stationed by the D.D.M.S. Corps as to be able to see all psychiatric cases evacuated by units in the corps area. A useful treatment centre lay-out consists of an admission and sorting section, a treatment section and a rehabilitation section. In the admission section a careful screening should be carried out with a view to the sifting out and evacuation of those who are unlikely to be returned to duty after a period of

10 to 14 days' treatment. A physical examination should be made in all cases, and a general explanation should be given to each patient about the causes of his breakdown and the steps it is proposed to take to effect a cure.

In the treatment section the aim is to give the patient good sleep free from anxiety. The dose of sedative required will vary according to the individual case. Routine dosage to all cases and over sedation should be avoided. The minimum necessary to produce good sleep is the optimum dosage. In very restless cases, a few c.c. of sodium pentothal intravenously followed by medinal by mouth may be useful. Sedation may be necessary for 24 to 36 hours. A full bladder is a common cause of sleep disturbance during this stage and must be avoided. A psychiatric interview should take place at the end of 48 or 72 hours when the effects of sedation have passed off. It is now usually possible to decide with more accuracy which cases will require longer treatment than is possible in a corps centre and these should be evacuated forthwith. Abreaction under intravenous barbiturate narcosis may exceptionally be of use in certain cases but, in general, those cases in which it is useful are not suitable for early return to combat duties.

The function of the rehabilitation section is to attempt to build up each man's confidence and to restore his personal pride. This is helped by talks with individual men, group discussions, physical training, etc. A daily programme something akin to that in a convalescent depot should be arranged. Supplies of fresh clothing must be at hand to replace torn soiled garments. A further psychiatric interview should take place about the seventh day, and a return to duty should be arranged at the earliest possible moment, which should be as soon as the man is fit to do so. If retained after this stage is reached, deterioration will often set in. Men returned fit for full combat duties should, if at all possible, be returned to their own units.

No fixed percentage of cases can be regarded as certain to return to front line duty after treatment in a corps centre. The percentage will depend on the effectiveness of the divisional exhaustion centres which normally should retain and treat men with a good prognosis for quick return to duty. Among those returned to front line duty from divisional and corps exhaustion centres, some relapses will undoubtedly occur but this is inevitable with any policy aiming at maximum conservation of manpower. In World War II, it was impossible to form any accurate estimate of relapses, but it was considered that over 80 per cent. of those returned to full combatant duty remained with their original units for at least six weeks. One divisional psychiatrist who remained with his division in India and Burma from 1943 until the end of the war in 1945, and consequently saw all psychiatric casualties from his division who were evacuated from the front, reported that the number of psychiatric casualties who broke down in battle after their return to duty was in the neighbourhood of 10 per cent. After the campaign was over, a follow up by this psychiatrist of psychiatric casualties he had previously returned to front line duty showed that approximately 6 or 7 per cent. were unfit to face further battle stress.

When divisional exhaustion centres are functioning effectively, though a varying percentage of men will still be returned to full combat duties from a corps exhaustion centre, some of those discharged to duty may require a lowering of medical category and a restriction of duties to L. of C. or base areas. The latter will normally be transferred from the corps exhaustion centre to a convalescent depot where lowering of medical category and re-allocation to suitable work can take place. Lowering of medical category will not normally be carried out at the corps exhaustion centre. Certain cases, although with a good prognosis for a return to duty, may require a longer period of rehabilitation than is possible in the limited period of stay allowed in a corps exhaustion centre. Such cases may be transferred to an army exhaustion centre for full rehabilitation.

TREATMENT AT ADVANCED BASE AND BASE LEVEL

Geographical and other factors such as a very long L. of C. will determine whether or not an advanced base psychiatric centre is established. This may be formed by either a psychiatric portion of a General Hospital, an advanced section of a Psychiatric General Hospital or an independent unit, but should, where possible, be adjacent to a General Hospital to which it may be attached for administrative purposes. A Convalescent Depot in this neighbourhood is essential. The advanced base psychiatric centre should cater for men who require up to 21 days' treatment in hospital and are likely to return to some form of duty after completion of treatment. Some may be expected to return to duty in their original medical category, but the majority will make an incomplete recovery and require down-grading in medical category and subsequent employment in L. of C. and base areas. If an advanced centre is established, the base centre should be confined to the treatment of the more severe cases and the holding of psychotics and others who are awaiting evacuation from the theatre.

The advanced base psychiatric centre ought not to be a medical centre in the accepted sense of the term. Medical officers in this centre ought not to be primarily concerned with treating symptoms. They should be concerned primarily with treating the main problem which is the patient's belief in his incapacity to fight. Any attempt by the patient to divert the medical officer to a prolonged discussion about symptoms should be avoided. Attempts, therefore, to treat patients by the usual methods carried out in civil practice are unfruitful. The aim of treatment of those who are likely to remain in the theatre—and only psychotics, mental defectives and exceptionally severe neurotics should be evacuated from the theatre—is to restore self confidence and reintegrate each man once again into a group so that his adjustment to others and to the Army will improve. **Impaired morale is the major factor in the majority: the will to fight as well as the capacity to fight has become impaired.** Emphasis must, therefore, be laid on the social aspects of treatment, and the whole organization of the advanced centre, and of the base centre, should an advanced centre not be opened, should have a predominantly military orientation. **Prolonged rest in comfortable base hospital surroundings is a big obstacle to recovery.** It is, therefore, necessary to provide an organisation in which men cease as far as possible to be regarded as hospital patients, but are placed under a much more military influence.

Two sets of machinery are required to deal with patients, one, to provide any specific psychiatric treatment necessary and the other to promote rehabilitation. The section of the advanced centre which is concerned with formal psychiatric treatment can be relatively small. Many admissions can often be immediately passed on to the rehabilitation section. Whatever form of psychiatric treatment is given, it should be completed within the minimum period of time, and no man who is likely to return to some form of duty in the theatre should normally require retention in the treatment section for a longer period than three weeks. Prolonged retention often leads to undesirable results. The nature of the treatment given in this section will depend to a large extent upon individual choice. Marked anxiety features are often amenable to narcosis over a period of from 4 to 7 days. Various techniques are available. The administration of a barbiturate with paraldehyde often gives good results. Narco-analysis is useful in the more severe dissociated cases. Dissociated features which do not respond to simple persuasion and suggestion can often be quickly removed and the factors underlying the breakdown more rapidly brought out. It is not, however, a panacea and its usefulness is limited. Pseudo-psychotic cases generally do not respond well to narco-analysis, and are often best treated by quiet reassurance with electro convulsive therapy in selected cases. An experienced mental nursing orderly may be of great assistance in bringing such a case again into contact with reality. Patients with psychosomatic symptoms increase in numbers in rear psychiatric centres. If treated early by a medical officer who has some knowledge of the principles of psychiatric treatment and who can explain the symptoms to the patient in simple terms and convince him, the results in cases of recent origin are often excellent. All too often, unfortunately, these cases are evacuated with a physical diagnosis, and subjected to prolonged

investigation in General Hospitals with the result that by the time
they come under psychiatric care their symptoms have become
fixed and they are lost for further combatant duty.

The rehabilitation section of the advanced base psychiatric centre
may be situated somewhere in the vicinity of the centre or it may
be possible to have it form an integral part of the centre itself.
The latter was achieved in the North West European Campaign
by the attachment to the psychiatric centre of the staff of one
company of a Convalescent Depot. This company took over the
rehabilitation programme in the centre and military rehabilitation
could then be instituted at the earliest possible stage. Something
akin to a Convalescent Depot programme was incorporated into the
psychiatric hospital and patients entered this as soon as fit to do so.
Each hospital ward represented a platoon under a senior N.C.O.
patient of the ward, and platoons were grouped into companies
under C.S.Ms. of the convalescent depot staff. Ward morale was
good. Well ordered ward routine gave the individual new admission
a measure of confidence and security and helped in the restoration
of his own diminished self-respect. Handling of patients in both
sections of the advanced psychiatric centre must be wise and
compassionate in a setting of strict military discipline. It must be
firm but just, and each individual patient must feel that he has
entered a progressive programme whose final aim is to return him
to duty. The bonds which bound him to his original unit have
weakened and he has dropped out. The aim of rehabilitation,
therefore, is to reintegrate him once again into a group and to
accept group and not individual aims. The whole programme must,
therefore, promote the factors which produce good group morale,
and the individual's absorption into a group must be carefully
supervised. He must be helped to feel secure in the company of
his fellows and to accept himself as having a duty to carry out.
This rehabilitation, however, is part of treatment and any break
in continuity must be avoided. If the rehabilitation centre is not
located in or adjoining the advanced base psychiatric centre, it
should have adequate psychiatric assistance available on its staff.
It may then be found useful to establish both an advanced and a
main rehabilitation centre. The advanced centre would provide a
short and vigorous rehabilitation solely for psychiatric casualties
from corps exhaustion centres and from the advanced base psychiatric
centre who were returning to duty in their original medical category.
No down-grading in medical category would be carried out. The
main rehabilitation centre would act as a receiving centre for
psychiatric casualties from forward and base treatment centres who
were fit for duty only in L. of C. and base areas. They would be
allocated to units direct from this centre and, therefore, would not
mix with reinforcements in transit camps and depots to the possible
detriment of the morale of the latter. The ordinary Convalescent

Depot has an almost insoluble problem if set the task of rehabilitating psychiatric casualties without adequate psychiatric assistance. The feeling among the staff tends to be that the psychiatric patients are cowards and " couldn't take it ". The patients, of course, take the opposite view, and finally antagonism may grow on this basis expressing itself among the staff in an increasing irritability, and amongst the patients in a growing sullenness and resentment. Treatment of psychiatric casualties in ordinary medical units throughout the chain of evacuation is likewise seldom successful. The correct curative atmosphere is seldom attained and patients become confirmed in the attitude that they are sick men.

The period of stay in the rehabilitation section of the centre should not normally exceed one month—it may well be much shorter—and all cases must be under psychiatric supervision to determine the earliest date when discharge to duty may be effected. Retention beyond this date frequently results in a deterioration. It is the responsibility of the medical officer to decide when the patient is fit to return to duty. Some patients may wish to argue this question and complain that they are still sick men. No useful result will follow if the medical officer counters this by such statements as : " Try going back to duty, and see if you can't carry on. If you can't make the grade, report sick." The patient merely accepts this as indicating that the medical officer is not quite certain about his fitness, and his will to carry on is weakened. Having made his decision, the medical officer should leave the patient in no doubt about it, and the decision should not be revised without very good reason. Ideally, the man when finally ready for discharge to duty should be discharged from the rehabilitation section direct to his new unit after any necessary alteration of medical category has been carried out. In practice, this is seldom possible and cases will then require to be discharged to a reinforcement holding unit, there to await posting to a unit. Prolonged holding of such men in holding units in an atmosphere of relative inactivity inevitably leads to a deterioration in morale. They are capable of doing excellent work, and, indeed, are often keen for some form of active work in an attempt to alleviate guilt feelings. Inactivity has often a most deleterious effect on their will to carry on. Medical officers at their new units should be instructed to treat them with benevolent firmness. They should not be regarded as semi-convalescents and entitled to special privileges and consideration.

APPENDIX 1

Divisional Exhaustion Centre	Corps Exhaustion Centre	Advanced base Psychiatric Centre	Base Psychiatric Centre
For treatment of mild cases likely to quickly return to full combatant duty.	For treatment of cases likely to quickly return to some form of duty.	For treatment of cases likely to return to some form of duty.	Mainly a holding centre for cases waiting evacuation to the U.K.
Located in the Rear Divisional Area usually in a F.D.S.	Located in the Corps Area usually in a F.D.S.	Located in L. of C. area in a psychiatric portion of a General Hospital or in advanced section of a Psychiatric Hospital.	Located in Base Area in a psychiatric portion of a General Hospital or in a Psychiatric Hospital.
Average stay up to 7 days.	Average stay up to 14 days.	Average stay up to approx. 42 days.	
Simple psychotherapeutic measures followed by a period of rehabilitation with group talks, physical training, simple organised amusements and games.	Simple psychotherapeutic measures followed by a period of rehabilitation with group talks, physical training, entertainment, organised games and sports.	Psychotherapeutic measures followed by a period of rehabilitation and training, etc.	
Approximately 60% likely to return to full combatant duty.	Varying percentage likely to return to full combatant duty. Majority of remainder to duty in L. of C. Area.	Varying percentage likely to return to full combatant duty, and great majority of remainder to duty in L. of C. or Base Areas.	

www.ingramcontent.com/pod-product-compliance
Lightning Source LLC
LaVergne TN
LVHW010307070426
835511LV00027B/3499